The Magical Teachings of Mr. Majestic

"I Don't Like Reading"

by Marcus L. Strother

Illustrated by N. Milano

The Magical Teachings of Mr. Majestic

This book is dedicated to my wife, who has believed in my every step.

You have believed that I could do things before I did.

Thank you for being my strength.

To Trinity, Marcus, and Christopher.

You are my highest achievement. I am because of you.

To my father, who seen my dream and helped me achieve it.

Your support has made this possible.

"All right class, it's time to read our first novel," said Mr. Majestic with enthusiasm in his voice.

Mr. Majestic was ready to start the first novel with his 6th grade class.

Immediately students in the class began to rumble.

"Aw Man, I don't like to read!"
This was all Mr. Majestic heard for the next 5 minutes.

Katy asked, "Mr. M., why do we have to read books, it's soooooo boring?"
Mr. Majestic stood at the front of his class scratching his head wondering what to do next.

Mr. Majestic went home and talked to his daughter Trinity about reading and she said she liked to read books about Oceans, because she wants to be a Marine Biologist.

She gave Mr. Majestic an idea!

Andre the chef, Katy the lawyer, Nicolas the construction worker, and Zion the entertainer were a few of the assigned careers.

Other students read through the next four passages and suddenly, from the corner of the room, Katy says, "Why can't we read that book Mr. M.? That sounds like a good book!"

The Magical Teachings of Mr. Majestic
Holding up the novel that he introduced earlier, Mr. Majestic says, "It's funny you asked that Katy. These passages are actually from this book!"

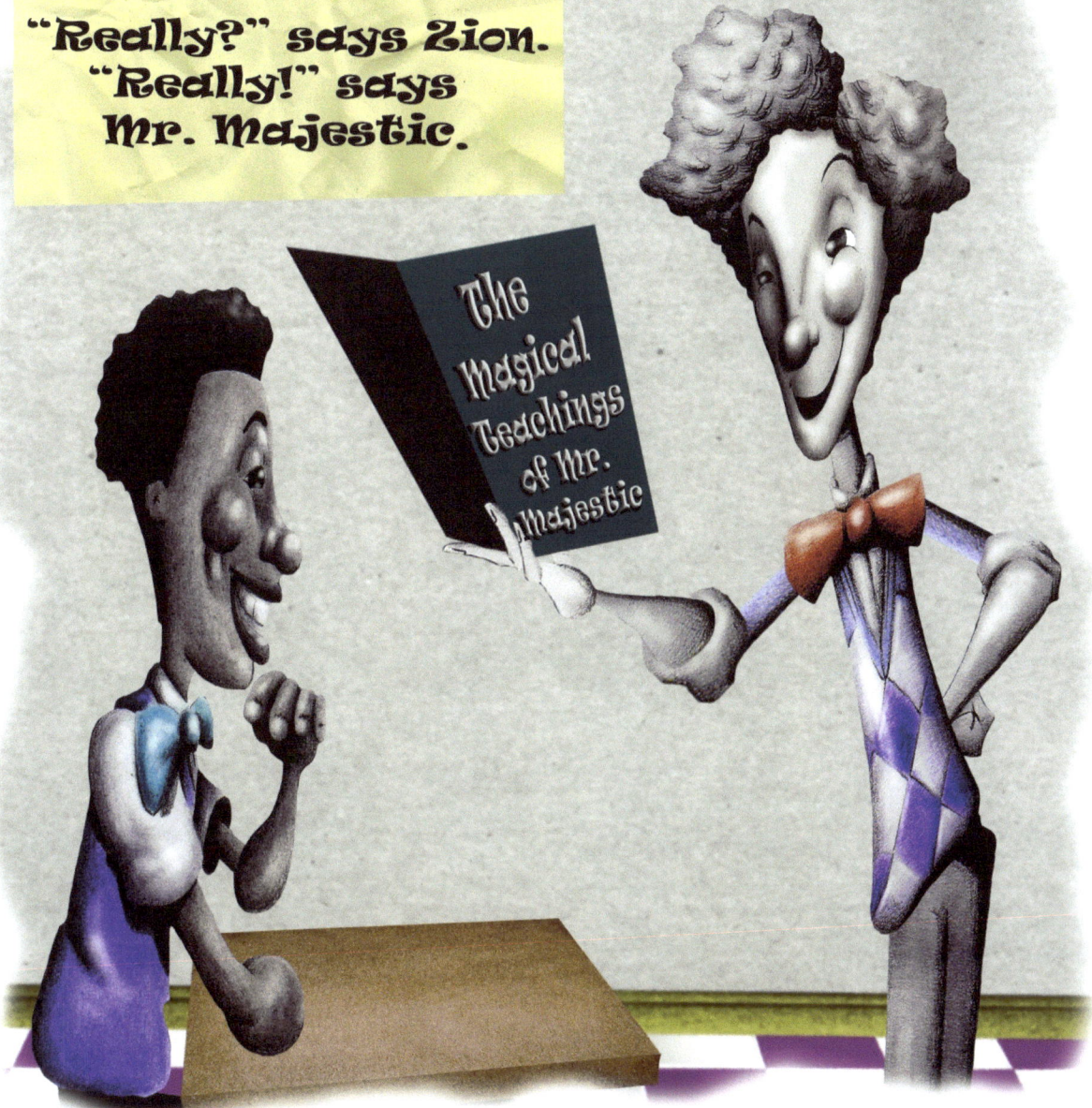

"Really?" says Zion.
"Really!" says
Mr. Majestic.

The Magical Teachings of Mr. Majestic

At that moment, the class began to get even more excited about reading their new novel and Mr. Majestic was able to start reading chapter one.

Later that night at home, Mr. Majestic kissed and hugged his three kids Trinity, Marcus, and Christopher and went to write in his journal.

Reading is a journey
a chance to go away
a chance to be a pirate
a football star today
a chance to be a hero
a Super or Batman
a chance to be a medieval knight
with a sword in both your hands
reading is a mystic journey
with magic in each phrase
from characters to settings
you'll find a brand new place
reading can be so much fun
from book to book to book
open one and look inside
to see what journeys next.

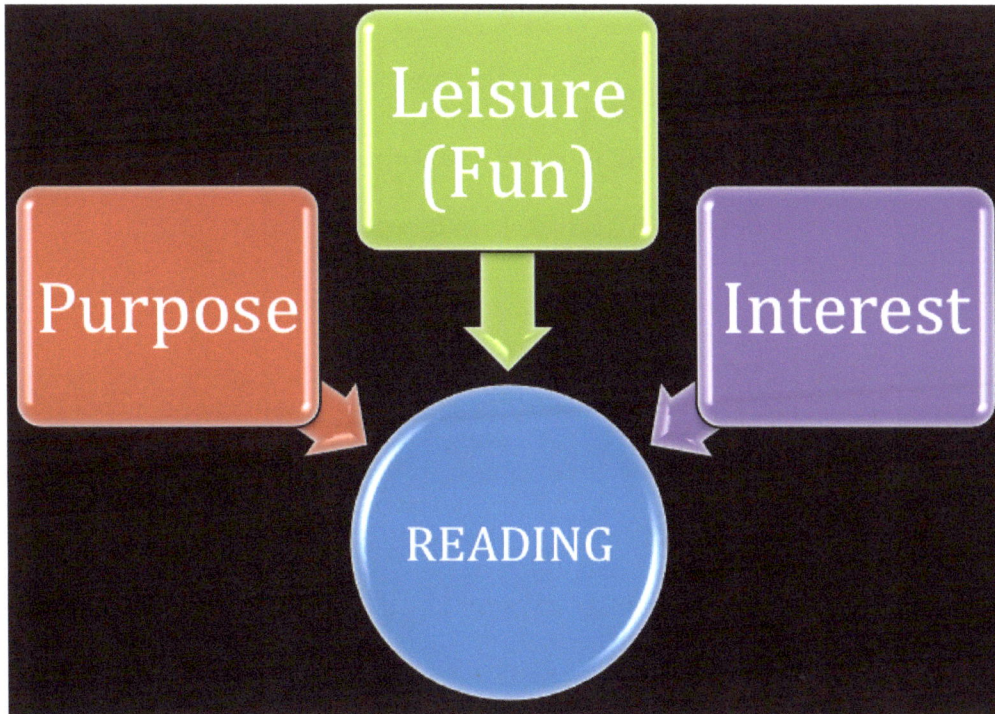

Purpose = School, Job requirement, etc.
Leisure (Fun)= Highlights for Kids, Discovery, etc.
Interest = Self-Help, Autobiography, etc.

Hello parents and students, I am Mr. Majestic and I want to first welcome you to my magical classroom. As you begin your journey, I want to spend a little time-sharing a few strategies that you can use at home.

Strategy #1 – "21 Minutes for 21 Days"

It is often stated that any habit can be formed if done for 21 days straight. We want reading to become a habit. Have your student sit down with you and read for 21 days. After those days have passed, start allowing your student to read independently.

Strategy #2 – "Show and Tell"

It is important for your student to see their parent is interested in their reading. Have your student read for you and when they have completed the reading, have them share with you what the story is about.

Strategy #3 – "MMR-Model More Reading"

Your student needs to see you model reading. Read with your student, read around your student, and read to your student. There will be nothing more important for your student then for them to see you modeling what it is that you expect them to do.

21Minutes for 21 Days

MMR=
Model
More
Reading

Show and Tell

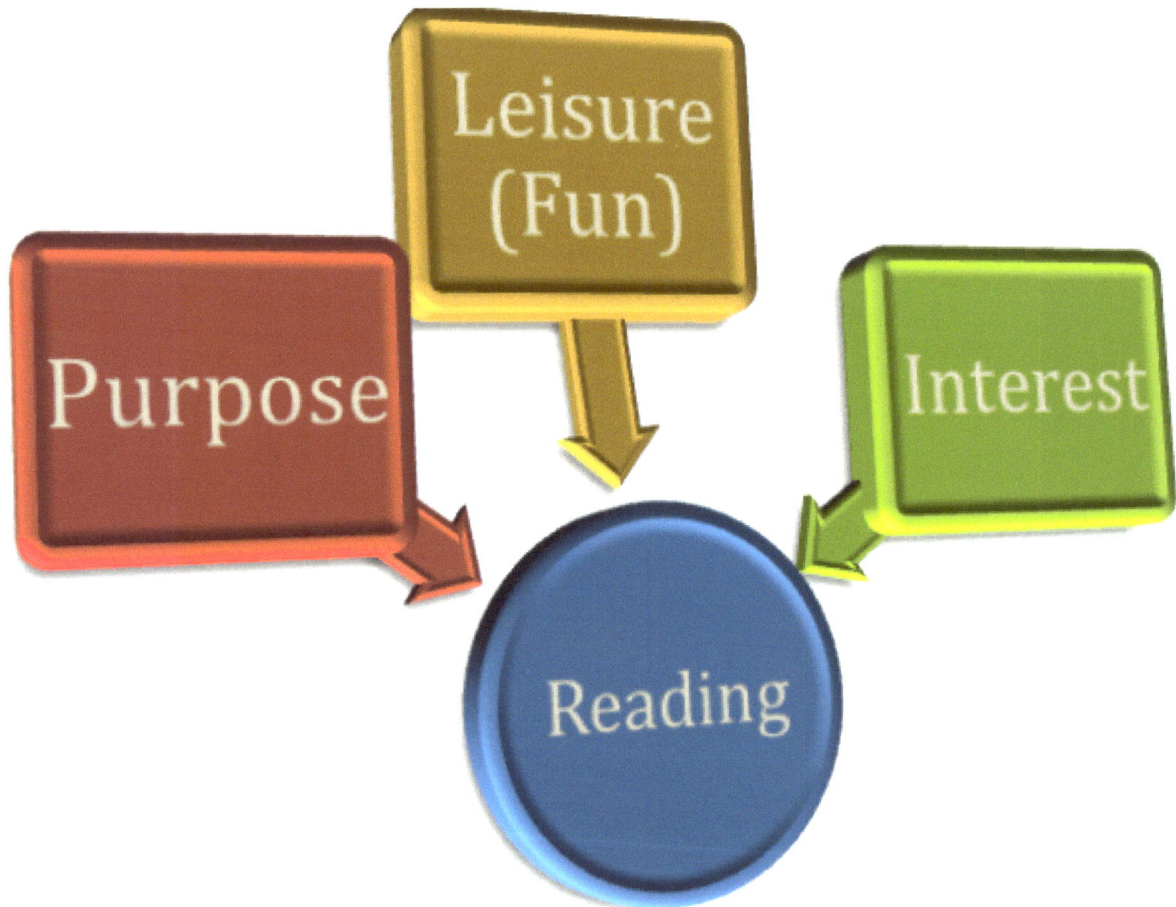

Purpose = School, Job requirement, etc.
Leisure (Fun)= Highlights for Kids, Discovery, etc.
Interest = Self-Help, Autobiography, etc.

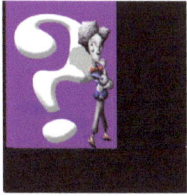

Hello fellow educators, I am Mr. Majestic and I want to first welcome you to my magical classroom. As you begin your journey, I want to spend a little time-sharing a few strategies that you can use in the classroom.

Strategy #1 – "D.E.A.R. (Drop Everything And Read) Day"

This can be an all day event. Spending the time to do this with your class helps your students understand the importance of reading. This is a day when students and teachers read for the entire day. Don't be afraid to allow the students to read as much as they want. Read, read, read!!!

Strategy #2 – "Parents Read Too"

At the beginning of the year, ask for parent volunteers who are willing to choose a book and spend a semester reading to the class. Bring your parent in weekly or bi-weekly to read, allow them to lead the class in discussion, and become a student to participate with your class in the reading.

Strategy #3 – "MMR-Model More Reading"

Your students need to see you model reading. Read with your students, read around your students, and read to your students. There will be nothing more important for your students then for them to see you modeling what it is that you expect them to do.

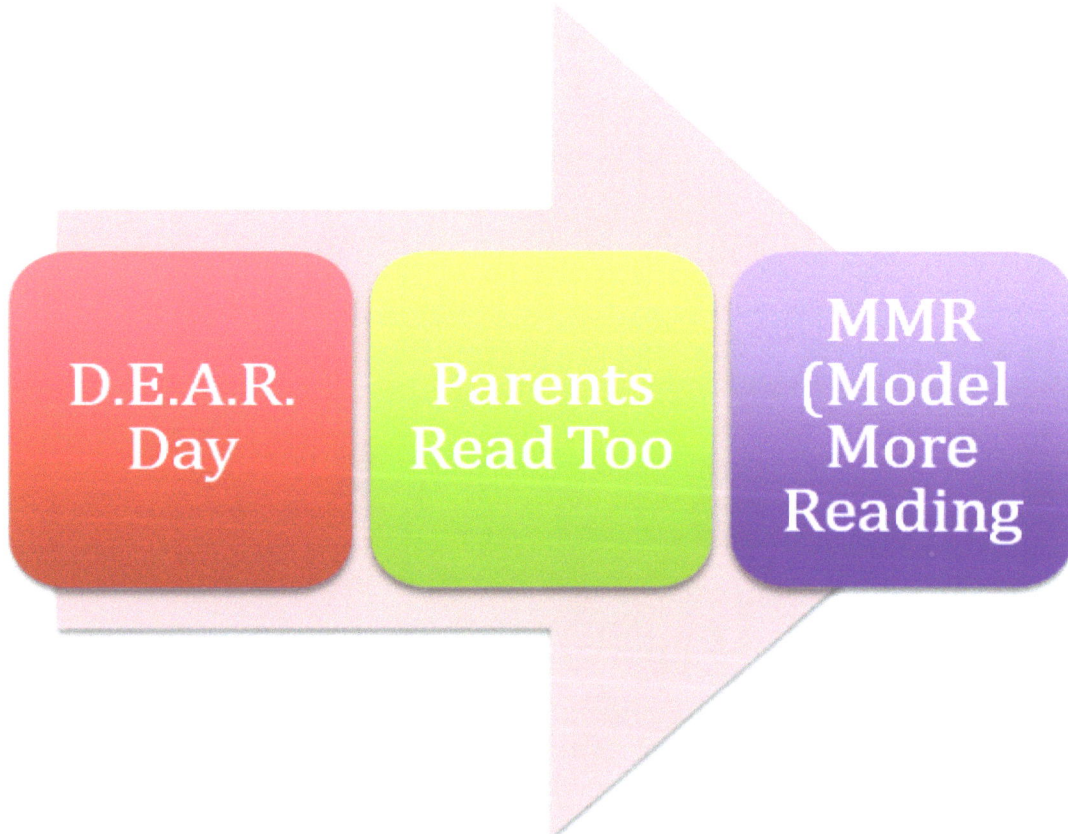

D.E.A.R. Day

Parents Read Too

MMR (Model More Reading)

www.ingramcontent.com/pod-product-compliance
Lightning Source LLC
Chambersburg PA
CBHW041557040426
42447CB00002B/205